Text compiled by Olivia Warburton
This edition copyright © 2005 Lion Hudson

A Lion Book
an imprint of
Lion Hudson plc
Mayfield House, 256 Banbury Road,
Oxford OX2 7DH, England
www.lionhudson.com
ISBN-13: 978-0-7459-5167-6
ISBN-10: 0-7459-5167-8

First edition 2005
10 9 8 7 6 5 4 3 2 1

Picture acknowledgments
Cover image and pp. 2–3, 17, 18, 23, 25, 29 copyright © Digital
Vision; pp. 6, 11 copyright © Geoff du Feu; pp. 8, 12 copyright
© David Alexander; p. 15 copyright © Tony Sweet/Digital Vision;
p. 21 copyright © ImageState; p. 26 copyright © Michael
Busselle/Digital Vision.

Text acknowledgments
p. 28: scripture quotation from the Good News Bible published
by The Bible Societies/HarperCollins Publishers, copyright ©
1966, 1971, 1976, 1992 American Bible Society. All other
scripture quotations taken from the *Holy Bible, New International
Version*, copyright © 1973, 1978, 1984 by International Bible
Society. Used by permission of Hodder & Stoughton Limited.
All rights reserved. 'NIV' is a registered trademark of International
Bible Society. UK trademark number 1448790.

Every effort has been made to trace and contact copyright owners
for material used in this book. We apologize for any inadvertent
omissions or errors, and would ask those concerned to contact us
so that full acknowledgment can be made in the future.

A catalogue record for this book is available
from the British Library

Typeset in 6/7 Berkeley OldStyle
Printed and bound in Singapore

To ....

From ....

A LION BOOK

Deep peace of the running wave to you,
deep peace of the flowing air to you,
deep peace of the quiet earth to you,
deep peace of the shining stars to you,
deep peace of the shades of night to you,
moon and stars always giving light to you,
deep peace of Christ, the Son of Peace, to you.

Celtic prayer

Peace I leave with you; my peace I give you.

John 14:27

For hope grew round me,
like the twining vine.

Samuel Taylor Coleridge

If it were not for hopes,
the heart would break.

Thomas Fuller

Every minute
life begins all over again.

Thomas Merton

Dear God, be good to me;
the sea is so large,
and my boat is so small.

Breton fisherman's prayer

For whatsoever from one place doth fall
Is with the tide unto another brought:
For there is nothing lost, that may be found,
if sought.

Edmund Spenser

Across the gateway of my heart
I wrote, 'No thoroughfare.'
But love came laughing by and cried,
'I enter everywhere.'

Herbert Shipman

And now these three remain:
faith, hope and love.
But the greatest of these is love.

1 Corinthians 13:13

*Faithless is he that says farewell
when the road darkens.*

J.R.R. Tolkien

*Come to me, all you who are weary
and burdened, and I will give you rest.*

Matthew 11:28

You never lose the love of God.

Jack Dominian

O God, grant us the serenity
to accept what cannot be changed,
the courage
to change what can be changed,
and the wisdom
to know the one from the other.

Reinhold Niebuhr

Serenity isn't freedom from the storm,
but peace within the storm.

Anon

*See how the farmer waits
for the land to yield its valuable crop
and how patient he is
for the autumn and spring rains.*

James 5:7

*Let nothing disturb you;
let nothing dismay you;
all things pass;
God never changes.*

St Teresa of Avila

There is a time for everything,
and a season for every activity under heaven:
a time to be born and a time to die,
a time to plant and a time to uproot,
a time to kill and a time to heal,
a time to tear down and a time to build,
a time to weep and a time to laugh,
a time to mourn and a time to dance.

Ecclesiastes 3:1–4

In spite of all,
Some shape of beauty moves away the pall
From our dark spirits.

John Keats

I don't envy those who have never known
any pain, physical or spiritual, because
I strongly suspect that the capacity for
pain and the capacity for joy are equal.
Only those who have suffered great pain
are able to know equally great joy.

Madeleine L'Engle

Even though I walk
through the valley of the shadow of death,
I will fear no evil,
for you are with me;
your rod and your staff,
they comfort me.
Surely goodness and love will follow me
all the days of my life,
and I will dwell in the house of the Lord
for ever.

Psalm 23:4, 6

*I believe in the sun
even when it is not shining.
I believe in love
even when I don't feel it.
I believe in God
even when he is silent.*

Words found written in a prison cell

*Expect the dawn of a new beginning
in the dark nights of life.*

Lloyd John Ogilvie

The mountains and hills may crumble,
but my love for you will never end.

Isaiah 54:10

My dearest Lord,
be thou a bright flame before me,
be thou a guiding star above me,
be thou a smooth path beneath me,
be thou a kindly shepherd behind me,
today and for evermore.

St Columba of Iona